Panini

Panini

whitecap

Notes

The American Egg Board advises that eggs should not be consumed raw. This book contains some dishes made with raw or lightly cooked eggs. It is prudent for more vulnerable people, such as pregnant and nursing mothers, the elderly, babies, and young children, to avoid uncooked or lightly cooked dishes made with eggs.

Meat and poultry should be cooked thoroughly. To test if poultry is cooked, pierce the flesh through the thickest part with a skewer or fork—the juices should run clear, never pink or red. Keep refrigerated until ready for cooking.

This book includes dishes made with nuts and nut derivatives. It is advisable for those with known allergic reactions to nuts and nut derivatives and those who may potentially be vulnerable to these allergies, such as pregnant and nursing mothers, the elderly, babies, and children, to avoid dishes made with nuts and nut oils. It is also prudent to check the labels of pre-prepared ingredients for the possible inclusion of nut derivatives.

This edition published in US and Canada by Whitecap Books. For more information, contact Whitecap Books, 351 Lynn Avenue, North Vancouver, British Columbia, Canada, V7J 2C4 www.whitecap.ca

First published in Great Britain in 2005 by Hamlyn, a division of Octopus Publishing Group Ltd, 2–4 Heron Quays, London E14 4JP

ISBN 1-55285-687-9

A CIP catalogue record for this book is available from the British Library

Printed and bound in China

10 9 8 7 6 5 4 3 2 1

contents

introduction

humble beginnings

These days sandwiches are seen as the quintessential lunchtime food. Quick to prepare, easy to eat, and filling, a sandwich can be eaten in a café, on the go, or even at your desk, depending on how much time you can spare for your midday meal. And now, instead of simply being made from a range of fillings inside plain white, sometimes wheat, sliced bread, there is an enormous choice of breads, with everything from tortillas and bagels to croissants and baguettes used to contain your choice of ingredients.

This wasn't always the case, however, and the sandwich had far more practical uses when it was on the menu in bygone years. In the Middle Ages, the sandwich bread was a substitute for a plate, and as such it was generally stale and tough, providing a firm surface on which to place the filling, which was the main part of the meal. Only the very hungry would consider eating the bread when they had eaten what was on it, and it was generally discarded. As bread came to be a staple food in many countries, it wasn't long before the sandwich began to bear more of a resemblance to what we eat today— providing a portable, substantial meal for farm workers and miners, among others—and it soon began to make an appearance in cafés and restaurants.

turn up the heat

The origins of the grilled sandwich can probably be traced to the Italian tradition of panini. Literally translated, *panino*

means roll or sandwich, and that's basically what they are. But they are actually far more than that, incorporating as they do a real sense of the Italian attitude to food—occasion, enjoyment, and indulgence. Panini tend to eschew the more traditional sandwich fillings elevating this popular morning snack and lunchtime fodder to greater heights, giving it a little more status.

The Italian attitude has spread, and now the grilled sandwich is usually regarded as something a little more refined than the ordinary, un-grilled sandwich. More unusual and expensive ingredients are often saved for this particular type of sandwich, which is really a way to enjoy a delicious meal without necessarily having to sit at a table and wait for something to be prepared.

back to basics

The essential requirements for successful panini are good-quality ingredients, and the Italian attitude has fortunately accompanied this hot snack on its travels around the world. If the bread is wonderfully fresh and fragrant, one or two good fillings can be sufficient to create a delicious sandwich. In Italy, cured meats, such as speck and prosciutto, may be used alone or combined with a local cheese, which is selected because the flavors complement each other.

As the trend for grilling sandwiches caught on elsewhere in the world, different interpretations of the traditional Italian snack developed, and panini are now a common item on café menus in many countries, with chefs creating signature sandwiches that can attract a loyal customer base.

Grilling transforms a regular sandwich into something entirely different, changing the texture and taste of both the bread and the filling. Although there are a number of specific sandwich grills on the market these days, most cafés use a regular sandwich grill and, depending on the type of bread they use, they may weigh this down with a heavy object while the sandwich is toasting. This compacts the bread and helps to make sure that the filling is piping

hot. It also ensures that the bread soaks up the delicious juices and flavors from the filling.

choosing bread

Most types of bread can be used to make panini, but before you choose remember that the bread and filling have to undergo quite a tough cooking process, often being pressed down with some force for several minutes. You should always try to choose a sturdy bread that isn't going to collapse or break up in the grill. Homemade breads are fine to use, and other suitable choices include bagels (plain or flavored), sourdough bread, pita bread, English muffins, and croissants. There are dozens of types of bread, however, and the best way to find your favorite combinations is through trial and error.

The bread that you choose will have a huge impact on the final flavor of your panini, and some breads are better suited to particular fillings. The recipes in this book have been designed around the breads that they use, and there are ideas for every meal, including some unusual sweet panini as well. For example, crêpes and panettone are ideal for sweet fillings, while baguettes and ciabatta are robust enough for strongly flavored ingredients. If you're using a highly textured or flavored bread, don't complicate it with too many competing flavors in the filling. It is important that every flavor is detectable and that the bread and filling work together to achieve an overall taste sensation.

the right ingredients

Once you realize that there are no limits to the fillings you can have in ordinary sandwiches, you will begin to appreciate the endless possibilities that panini can offer. They can be as simple or as complicated as you want, and they are suitable for a quick snack while you're on the move or for a real treat to be savored. There are, of course, many tried-and-true combinations that work especially well in panini, and you'll find many of these on the pages that follow.

cheese Because panini are grilled, some cheeses are perfect—fontina, haloumi, mozzarella, and goat cheese are just a few of the cheeses that take well to grilling. They melt gently and warm through, without losing their shape or becoming too runny.

chicken This is a good accompaniment for other complementary flavors, and it is delicious when served hot in a sandwich. Look for the Thai Red Chicken on page 73, which is served with cashew satay sauce.

ham Cured ham works especially well in panini and was a traditional ingredient in the original Italian panini. The strong flavors are not overwhelmed by the bread that surrounds

the meat or by the other ingredients that you use. Bacon is also a great panini filling, and can be combined with eggs to make a substantial breakfast. See the Bacon 'n' Eggs Muffin Brunch on page 14.

sauces Use your favorite sauces with all types of panini fillings. Chutney, relish, flavored mayonnaise, and mustard can all be added to your panini, or try something a little bit different like tapenade, as in the Haloumi with Tapenade and Scallions (Green Onions) on page 28.

vegetables A wide range of vegetables can be used in panini, but bell peppers, zucchini, and onions are popular choices. Cook them quickly first if you want. Several of the recipes in this book are appropriate for vegetarians, including more unusual ideas such as Brie, Peach, and Watercress (page 32) and Roasted Chickpea and Tomato Salsa (page 38).

top tips for homemade panini

Preparing and eating food should be an enjoyable experience, and panini are no exception. Here is an opportunity to be creative and to embrace the challenge of turning the humble sandwich into a delicious gastronomic masterpiece.

Although practice makes perfect, there are a few guidelines that will help you to be certain that your panini turn out exactly as you wish.

• Make sure all your ingredients are ready before you begin. Once you start assembling your panini, you don't want to be rushing around looking for half the ingredients. If bell peppers need to be grilled or chicken cooked, do it in advance. Consider using your sandwich grill to do so.

• Make sure your grill is hot enough to use before you put your panini on the plate. If you have a proper sandwich or panini grill, the light will indicate when it's hot enough to use. Be vigilant and lift the grill plate occasionally during cooking to check on your panini—you don't want them sitting on a lukewarm grill or burning because you've left them to cook for too long.

• Don't pack too many ingredients into your panini or they will spill out of the bread and burn on the grill. That doesn't mean you can't use a good selection of ingredients, but take care not to use too much of each. The panini will also be difficult and messy to eat if the filling is oozing out of it.

special equipment

If you have a well-equipped kitchen, you shouldn't need to buy anything special to create gourmet snacks. A sandwich grill is essential if you're going to be making a lot of panini, although it is possible to cook them in a ridged grill pan as long as you press down hard with a metal spatula. If you're

a committed sandwich griller, you might want to invest in a panini press, a specially designed grill that can usually cook two panini at once.

You will need a spatula to remove your panini from the grill so that they don't break up or lose any of the filling. Use a sharp knife to cut them in half before serving.

Nonstick cooking spray is ideal for grilling panini and is a healthier option than bottled oil. It gives a light coating of oil, which will prevent the bread from sticking to the grill, but it won't make the panini greasy.

So, with the pantry well stocked and the sandwich grill preheated and ready to use, the only thing remaining is for you to pick out your first recipe and start creating some wonderful panini. Be careful, however—once you start you may become addicted!

start the day right

gravlax with cream cheese and chives

2 poppy and sesame seed bagels, cut
  in half horizontally
4 oz cream cheese
6 oz gravlax, finely sliced
2 tablespoons snipped chives
black pepper, plus extra to serve
warmed hollandaise sauce, to serve

Serves 2
Preparation time 4 minutes
Cooking time 4–6 minutes

1 Place the bagels, cut side down, on a sandwich grill. Without closing the lid, leave them to toast for 2–3 minutes until golden. Remove from the grill. Spread the bases with the cream cheese and then top with the gravlax. Scatter the snipped chives over the bagel and season with black pepper.

2 Top with the lids and return to the sandwich grill. Lower the top plate and toast for 2–3 minutes, or according to the manufacturer's instructions, until golden and crispy. Serve immediately with warmed hollandaise sauce and a sprinkling of black pepper.

bacon 'n' eggs muffin brunch

2 large eggs
2 portabella mushroom caps, trimmed
2 pork sausages, sliced in half
     lengthwise
2 small tomatoes, halved
4 slices Irish-style bacon
2 English muffins, cut in half
     horizontally
4 thin slices of Cheddar cheese
     (optional)

To serve
mini hash browns
steak sauce or ketchup
large mug of tea or coffee

Serves 2
Preparation time 8 minutes
Cooking time 10–12 minutes

This hearty breakfast should keep you going until dinner time! In this recipe a sandwich grill is used both to cook the breakfast ingredients and to toast the finished muffin.

1 Heat the sandwich grill and gently crack the eggs directly onto the bottom plate. Once the white is cooked but the yolk still has some "wobble," carefully remove the eggs from the heat and set aside. Place the mushrooms on the bottom plate along with the sausages, tomatoes, and bacon. Remove each ingredient from the heat as soon as it is cooked and set aside to keep warm. Wipe the sandwich grill with a damp cloth.

2 Stack the cooked ingredients on the base of the English muffins, ending with the eggs followed by the slices of Cheddar (if using). Cover with the lids and toast in the sandwich grill for 2–3 minutes, or according to the manufacturer's instructions, until the muffins are hot and golden.

3 Serve immediately with mini hash browns and steak sauce or ketchup and a large mug of steaming tea or coffee.

ricotta and pear drizzle

1/2 cup ricotta cheese
4 thick slices of all-butter brioche
1 small, sweet dessert pear, cored and
   finely sliced
1/4 cup runny honey, plus extra for
   drizzling

Serves 2
Preparation time 3 minutes
Cooking time 1–2 minutes

Whether you are planning a lazy day or are in the mood for a special treat, this mouth-watering breakfast combination is perfection itself.

1 Spread the ricotta thickly over two slices of brioche and fan out the pear slices over the top. Drizzle with the honey and top with the remaining slices of brioche.

2 Toast in a sandwich grill for 1–2 minutes, or according to the manufacturer's instructions, until the bread is crisp and golden. Cut in half diagonally and serve immediately, drizzled with extra honey.

taleggio and wild mushrooms

2 tablespoons butter
2 tablespoons olive oil
3 oz mixed wild mushrooms, trimmed
1 small garlic clove, chopped
2 tablespoons roughly chopped parsley
2 large, all-butter croissants
3 1/2 oz taleggio cheese, sliced
salt and pepper

Serves 2
Preparation time 6 minutes
Cooking time 6–8 minutes

Some sandwich grills have a "melt" setting on them, which means that you can stop the top grill from coming all the way down. This enables you to make open melted sandwiches, which is perfect for this recipe. If your sandwich grill doesn't have this setting, just put the lids on the sandwiches and cook them like regular grilled sandwiches. Alternatively, finish them off under a hot broiler.

1 Melt the butter with the olive oil in a frying pan. Add the mushrooms, garlic, and parsley and fry over medium heat until soft and golden. Season well, remove from the heat, and allow to cool.

2 Split the croissants in half horizontally and top the bases with the taleggio and sautéed wild mushrooms.

3 Set the sandwich grill to "melt," place the croissants on the bottom plate, and lower the top so that it stops just before it touches the cheese. This will toast the bases of the croissants and gently melt the topping. Remove from the panini grill and serve immediately.

banana and peanut butter

2 cinnamon and raisin bagels,
   cut in half horizontally
1/2 cup peanut butter, smooth
   or crunchy
1 large banana, sliced

To serve
grape jelly
hot chocolate
whipped cream

Serves 2
Preparation time 2 minutes
Cooking time 4–6 minutes

1 Place the bagels cut side down on a sandwich grill to toast for 2–3 minutes, without lowering the top plate.

2 Remove the bagels from the sandwich grill and spread the bases generously with your choice of peanut butter.

3 Arrange the banana slices over the top and cover with the lids. Toast in the sandwich grill for 2–3 minutes, or according to the manufacturer's instructions, until crisp and golden.

4 Serve immediately with grape jelly, a steaming mug of hot chocolate, and a bowl of whipped cream.

oat and apple fruesli

A perfect start to your morning, this wholesome breakfast alternative will leave you feeling virtuous all day long!

1 Mix together all the dry ingredients in a bowl and stir in the apple juice and Greek yogurt until well coated. Spoon onto two slices of cinnamon raisin bread and place the remaining two slices on top.

2 Toast in a sandwich grill for 2–3 minutes, or according to the manufacturer's instructions, until crisp and golden. Serve immediately with an extra bowl of Greek yogurt and a glass of apple juice.

1/4 cup rolled oats
1/4 cup rolled wheat flakes
2 tablespoons sunflower seeds
2 tablespoons sweetened puffed
   quinoa
1 dried, ready-to-eat banana
2 dried, ready-to-eat apricots
5 slices crisp, dried apple, crumbled
1/4 cup golden raisins
2 tablespoons dried, shaved coconut
   (optional)
2 tablespoons light brown sugar
1/4 cup apple juice
1/4 cup Greek yogurt, plus extra to
serve
4 large slices of cinnamon raisin bread
glass of apple juice, to serve

Serves 2
Preparation time 8 minutes
Cooking time 2–3 minutes

brunch croque monsieur

4 thick slices of French country bread

2 tablespoons melted butter

1/4 cup finely grated Parmesan cheese

2 large slices of country-style roast
ham

1 cup Emmental or similar Swiss
cheese, coarsely grated

fried egg (optional, for croque
madame)

Serves 2
Preparation time 8 minutes
Cooking time 5 minutes

Bring a little taste of France to your brunch table with this bistro favorite.
The grated Parmesan coating gives the toast an irresistible crunch. Top with
a perfect fried egg for a brunch croque madame.

1 Brush one side of each slice of country bread with the melted butter using a
pastry brush and sprinkle with the Parmesan. Making sure that the Parmesan
coated sides are on the outside, lay down two slices of bread and top each with
a slice of ham and half the coarsely grated Emmental.

2 Top with the remaining two slices of bread and toast in a sandwich grill for
4–5 minutes, or according to the manufacturer's instructions, until the bread
is golden and crispy and the Emmental is beginning to ooze from the sides.

3 Serve immediately. Top the sandwich with a fried egg if you wish to make
it into a brunch croque madame.

herby scrambled eggs with melted gruyère

3 large eggs

1/3 cup milk

dash of Tabasco sauce

2 tablespoons finely chopped chives

2 tablespoons finely chopped chervil

1 teaspoon finely chopped tarragon

2 tablespoons butter

4 thick slices of sourdough bread

3/4 cup finely grated sharp Gruyère
   cheese

salt and pepper

crispy bacon strips, to serve (optional)

Serves 2

Preparation time 8 minutes

Cooking time 8 minutes

1 Lightly beat the eggs in a bowl with the milk, Tabasco sauce, the herbs, and salt and pepper to taste. Melt the butter in a nonstick pan over medium heat. When the butter is beginning to froth, pour in the egg mixture and stir gently with a fork. Allow to cook slowly, stirring occasionally, until the eggs are almost cooked. Remove from the heat. Add more salt and pepper to taste, if needed.

2 Spoon the scrambled egg mixture onto two slices of sourdough bread and sprinkle with the grated Gruyère. Top with the remaining slices of bread and toast in a sandwich grill for 2–3 minutes, or according to the manufacturer's instructions, until the bread is golden and crisp. Serve immediately with strips of crispy bacon, if using.

spanish frittata

1/4 cup olive oil

1 small red onion, halved and cut into strips

4 oz cold, cooked potatoes, thickly sliced

2 oz finely sliced chorizo sausage, shredded (optional)

3 oz roasted red bell peppers, cut into strips

1 garlic clove, crushed

1/2 teaspoon paprika

1/4 cup roughly chopped flat leaf parsley

2 teaspoons chopped marjoram

3 large eggs, lightly beaten

1/2 cup grated Cheddar cheese

8 slices of multigrain bread

salt and pepper

Serves 4
Preparation time 10 minutes
Cooking time 15–18 minutes

The sun is shining and summer is just around the corner. This sandwich is for those long, lazy Sunday breakfasts that last until lunchtime.

1 Heat the olive oil in a small frying pan. Add the onion and fry over medium heat until it is softened and golden. Add the potatoes and fry until they are hot and golden. Add the chorizo (if using), bell peppers, garlic, paprika, and herbs, and stir with a spatula. Add the eggs and some seasoning and allow the mixture to cook until the eggs set, stirring occasionally to prevent the mixture from sticking.

2 Scatter the Cheddar over the frittata and place the frying pan under a preheated broiler until the cheese is melted and bubbling. Remove and leave to cool. Once the frittata is cool enough to handle, cut it into quarters and place each wedge on a slice of multigrain bread. Top with the remaining bread slices to form four sandwiches and toast in a sandwich grill for 2–3 minutes, or according to the manufacturer's instructions, until the bread is golden and crispy.

best vegetarian
sandwich

grilled sweet potato and blue cheese

1/4 cup honey

1 teaspoon crushed red pepper flakes

1/4 cup sesame oil

1/2 cup olive oil

1 large sweet potato, peeled and
   thickly sliced

1/2 cup sugar-snap peas

2 potato cakes

2 oz blue cheese, such as Roquefort

salt and pepper

Serves 2
Preparation time 5 minutes
Cooking time 12 minutes

Potato cakes are a traditional Irish food and are available in supermarkets and Irish specialist food stores. If you can't find potato cakes, pita bread makes a good substitute in this recipe.

1 Combine the honey, red pepper flakes, sesame oil, and olive oil in a small bowl. Place the sweet potato slices and sugar-snap peas in a large bowl and toss them with half of the honey dressing until they are evenly coated. Season well and place on a baking sheet, arranging the vegetables so that the potatoes are in a single layer. Place them under a hot broiler for 8 minutes, turning occasionally with tongs until the potatoes are soft and turning golden.

2 When they are cool enough to handle, arrange the potato slices and peas over half the base of each potato cake and crumble the blue cheese over them. Fold the potato cakes to create two sandwiches and toast in a sandwich grill for 3–4 minutes, or according to the manufacturer's instructions, until the bread is golden and the cheese is just melting. Serve immediately with a small bowl of the remaining honey dressing to drizzle.

haloumi with tapenade and scallions (green onions)

6 oz haloumi cheese, thickly sliced

1/4 cup black olive tapenade

2 individual Turkish breads, cut in half horizontally

2 scallions (green onions), chopped

finely grated zest of 1/2 lemon

1/4 cup roughly chopped flat leaf parsley

olive oil, to drizzle

lemon wedges, to garnish

Serves 2
Preparation time 3 minutes
Cooking time 5 minutes

Turkish bread is deliciously fluffy and about 1 inch thick. If you can't get hold of it, semolina bread will do just as well, or try lavash, a Middle-Eastern bread, which makes more of a wrap.

1 Preheat the sandwich grill and lay the haloumi slices directly on the bottom plate, without bringing down the top plate. Cook for about 2 minutes, until the bottom is golden. Remove and set aside.

2 Spread the tapenade over the bottom halves of the Turkish breads and top with the cheese. Sprinkle with the scallions (green onions), lemon zest, and parsley, and drizzle with olive oil.

3 Top with the lids and toast in the sandwich grill for 2–3 minutes, or according to the manufacturer's instructions, until the bread is golden and crispy. Serve immediately garnished with lemon wedges.

lemony mozzarella and parmesan

4 slices of poppy seed bread, or 2 poppy seed rolls, cut in half horizontally

1/2 cup finely grated Parmesan cheese

2 tablespoons capers, rinsed

1/4 cup pine nuts, lightly toasted

finely grated zest of 1 lemon

4 oz mozzarella cheese, sliced

handful of arugula leaves

2 tablespoons lemon juice

salt and pepper

Serves 2
Preparation time 6 minutes
Cooking time 2–3 minutes

1 Sprinkle two slices of poppy seed bread with half the Parmesan and scatter the capers, pine nuts, and lemon zest on top. Arrange the mozzarella slices over the top and scatter the arugula leaves over them. Drizzle with lemon juice, season well, and sprinkle with the remaining Parmesan.

2 Top with the lids and toast in a sandwich grill for 2–3 minutes, or according to the manufacturer's instructions, until the bread is toasted and the melted mozzarella is oozing from the sides.

ricotta and roasted vegetable

1 red onion, cut into quarters

1 eggplant, sliced

1 yellow bell pepper, halved, cored, and seeded

1 red bell pepper, halved, cored, and seeded

2 small zucchini, sliced lengthwise

1/2 cup olive oil

1 small, round country-style loaf

1 small bunch of basil, leaves stripped

2/3 cup ricotta cheese

salt and pepper

herby salad leaves, to serve

Serves 2
Preparation time 10 minutes
Cooking time 30 minutes

A pan-bagnat *is a kind of stuffed picnic loaf. The best kind of bread to use for this recipe is a small, round, flattish country-style loaf.*

1 Arrange the vegetables in a large roasting pan, drizzle with 1/3 cup of the olive oil, add plenty of salt and pepper and cook in a preheated 400° oven for 25 minutes or until they are soft and golden.

2 Slice the top off the small loaf and pull most of the dough from inside the bottom half. Adding basil leaves as you work, layer about half the roasted vegetables inside the loaf, add the ricotta, and top with the remaining vegetables. Drizzle with the remaining oil and top with the lid.

3 Toast in a sandwich grill for 5–6 minutes, or according to the manufacturer's instructions, until the bread is toasted and the filling is hot. Cut into wedges and serve immediately with a herby salad.

roasted red pepper and feta

2 red bell peppers, cut in half
   lengthwise, cored and seeded
3 oz feta cheese, sliced
1 teaspoon dried oregano
1 teaspoon finely grated lemon zest
1/4 cup olive oil
2 tablespoons balsamic vinegar
2 tablespoons pesto sauce
2 pieces of foccacia, cut in half
   horizontally
small handful of red chard leaves
salt and pepper

Serves 2
Preparation time 6 minutes
Cooking time 34 minutes

1 Place the peppers cut side up in a roasting pan and place the feta slices inside each half. Scatter with the oregano and lemon zest and season well. Drizzle with the olive oil and balsamic vinegar and cook in a preheated 350° oven for 25–30 minutes, until the peppers are softened and starting to blacken around the edges. Remove and set aside to cool.

2 Spread the pesto over the bases of the foccacia and arrange the chard leaves on top. Layer the peppers over the chard and top with the lids. Toast in a sandwich grill for 3–4 minutes, until the bread is golden and the leaves are wilted.

brie, peach, and watercress

3 1/2 oz firm Brie, sliced
1 small baguette, cut in half and sliced
    in half horizontally
1 peach, pitted and sliced
1 small bunch of watercress
pepper
2 tablespoons olive oil

Serves 2
Preparation time 3 minutes
Cooking time 2–3 minutes

1 Arrange the sliced Brie over the bases of the baguette halves and top with the peach slices. Scatter the watercress leaves over the peaches and grind black pepper over them. Drizzle with olive oil and top with the lids.

2 Toast in a sandwich grill for 2–3 minutes, or according to the manufacturer's instructions, until the bread is crispy and the cheese is beginning to ooze. Serve immediately.

spinach, blue cheese, and walnuts

1 1/2 cups baby spinach leaves
4 thick slices of rustic bread
3 oz Roquefort cheese, sliced
1/4 cup walnut halves
2 tablespoons olive oil
pepper

To serve
1 pear, sliced
large handful of watercress

Serves 2
Preparation time 4 minutes
Cooking time 5–6 minutes

1 Arrange the spinach leaves evenly over two slices of rustic bread. Scatter the Roquefort over it, followed by the walnut halves. Drizzle with the olive oil and season with freshly ground black pepper.

2 Place the tops on the sandwiches and place them in a sandwich grill. Bring down the top and toast for 5–6 minutes, or according to the manufacturer's instructions, until the bread is golden and the cheese has melted.

3 Cut each sandwich in half and serve immediately with slices of pear and a large handful of watercress.

vegetarian quesadilla

1/4 cup refried beans

4 taco-size tortillas

1 cup cooked long-grain white rice

1 red bell pepper, cored, seeded, and
finely sliced

1 onion, finely sliced

2/3 cup pinto beans, cooked and
drained

1/4 cup salsa

1 large tomato, seeded and sliced

2 jalapeño peppers, sliced (optional)

3 oz Monterey Jack cheese, sliced

To serve
sour cream
guacamole

Serves 2
Preparation time 5 minutes
Cooking time 3–4 minutes

1 Spread the refried beans over half of each tortilla and spoon the cooked rice
over them. Scatter with the red bell pepper and onion and then the pinto beans.
Spoon on the salsa and top with the tomato and jalapeño peppers (if using), and
finish with the sliced Monterey Jack.

2 Fold the tortillas in half and toast in a sandwich grill for 3–4 minutes, or according
to the manufacturer's instructions, until they are crispy and the filling is hot and
melted. Serve immediately with sour cream and guacamole.

potato and onion blinis

1/2 cup olive oil

1 small red onion, finely sliced

21/2 cups grated potato

pinch of dried thyme

4 large blinis

1/4 cup mascarpone cheese, plus extra
to serve

1/4 cup oil-cured, pitted black olives,
halved

salt and pepper

Serves 2
Preparation time 8 minutes
Cooking time 12–13 minutes

1 Heat the olive oil in a large frying pan over medium heat. Add the onion and grated potato and fry gently for 10 minutes, turning frequently, until golden and crispy. Stir in the thyme, season well, and remove from the heat.

2 Spread the bases of two blinis with the mascarpone and carefully spoon the potato mixture over it. Scatter with the olives and top with the remaining blinis.

3 Toast the blinis in a sandwich grill for 2–3 minutes, or according to the manufacturer's instructions, until they are golden and crispy and the filling is hot. Serve immediately with extra mascarpone.

double goat cheese and asparagus

5 oz trimmed asparagus spears
2 tablespoons olive oil
4 oz soft mild goat cheese
4 slices of French-style walnut bread
3 oz firm goat cheese with rind, sliced
1 teaspoon lemon thyme leaves
salt and pepper

To serve
large handful of arugula leaves
2 teaspoons truffle oil

Serves 2
Preparation time 5 minutes
Cooking time 18–20 minutes

This combination of warm, melting goat cheese on hot, crispy bread is inspired by the French salade au chèvre chaud.

1 Toss the asparagus spears in the olive oil, season well, and place in a roasting pan. Cook them in a preheated 350° oven for about 15 minutes, until golden.

2 Spread the soft goat cheese over two slices of walnut bread. Top with the roasted asparagus spears and arrange the sliced goat cheese over them.

3 Scatter with the lemon thyme leaves, top with the remaining slices of bread, and toast in a sandwich grill for 3–4 minutes, or according to the manufacturer's instructions, until the bread is golden and the cheese has melted. Serve immediately scattered with arugula leaves and a drizzle of truffle oil.

crispy camembert

1/3 cup fresh breadcrumbs
2 tablespoons chopped chervil
1 teaspoon finely grated lemon zest
4 oz Camembert cheese, thickly sliced
1/4 cup vegetable oil
1/4 cup fruity mango chutney
2 small, individual naan breads, cut in
   half horizontally
1 scallion (green onion), sliced
salt and pepper

Serves 2
Preparation time 10 minutes
Cooking time 6 minutes

The sweet, fruity flavor of mango chutney cuts through the richness of the Camembert cheese in this tasty recipe.

1 Combine the breadcrumbs, chervil, and lemon zest in a bowl with some salt and pepper. Transfer to a plate and press the Camembert slices into the breadcrumb mix, making sure they are thoroughly coated.

2 Heat the oil in a small frying pan and fry the cheese for 3–4 minutes until golden and crispy. Remove from the pan and drain any excess oil on paper towels. Spread the mango chutney over the bases of the naan breads and scatter the sliced scallion (green onion) over it. Arrange the crispy Camembert over the onion and top with the lids.

3 Toast in a sandwich grill for 2 minutes, or according to the manufacturer's instructions, until the bread is hot and crispy. Cut in half and serve immediately.

roasted chickpea and tomato salsa

2 garlic and herb naan breads, cut in half horizontally

Salsa
1 14-oz can chickpeas, drained and rinsed
1/4 cup olive oil
1 teaspoon cumin seeds, toasted
1/2 teaspoon smoked paprika
2 plum tomatoes, seeded and chopped
1 small red onion, halved and finely sliced
1 garlic clove, chopped
3/4-inch cube fresh root ginger, peeled and finely shredded
salt and pepper

Serves 2
Preparation time 8 minutes
Cooking time 28 minutes

This recipe contains a delicious smoky chickpea and tomato salsa, full of garlic and ginger flavors, which is roasted before being used as a filling for an irresistible toasted sandwich.

1 Toss the salsa ingredients together and place them in a large roasting pan. Cook in a preheated 425° oven for 25 minutes, until the salsa is sticky and golden.

2 Remove the salsa from the oven and spoon onto the bases of the naan breads. Top with the lids and toast in a sandwich grill for 2–3 minutes, or according to the manufacturer's instructions, until the bread is golden and crispy. Cut into wedges and serve immediately.

toasting the catch

herby swordfish *a la plancha*

2 swordfish steaks, about 6 oz each

2 tablespoons olive oil

2 tablespoons chopped oregano

2 teaspoons chopped thyme

finely grated zest of 1 lemon

2 tablespoons pine nuts, lightly toasted

2 tablespoons capers, rinsed

2 sun-dried tomato ciabatta rolls, cut in
   half horizontally

2 teaspoons harissa paste

large handful of arugula leaves

salt and pepper

Serves 2
Preparation time 8 minutes
Cooking time 6 minutes

The term a la plancha *is used to describe something that is cooked on a griddle, but in this recipe it is the plates of the sandwich grill that first cook the swordfish, and then the sandwich itself, showing how versatile it can be. If you can't find swordfish, tuna makes a good substitute in this recipe.*

1 Rub the swordfish steaks with the olive oil, chopped herbs, and grated lemon zest, then season well with salt and pepper.

2 Heat the sandwich grill and place the swordfish inside, bringing down the top plate. Cook for about 2 minutes and then remove the fish. Wipe the machine with a damp cloth.

3 Scatter the pine nuts and capers over the base of each ciabatta roll. Lay the swordfish steaks on top, then spread a thin layer of harissa on the lids and place them on top of the sandwiches.

4 Toast the sandwiches in the clean sandwich grill for about 4 minutes, or according to the manufacturer's instructions, until the bread is hot. Remove from the sandwich grill and add the arugula leaves. Serve immediately.

tuna, pesto, and mozzarella

1/4 cup red pesto sauce

2 large ciabatta rolls, cut in half
  horizontally

1 5-oz can tuna in olive oil, drained

2 oz boccocini (baby mozzarella), cut
  in half

2 teaspoons olive oil

1 teaspoon balsamic vinegar

6 large basil leaves

1/3 cup sun-dried tomatoes

Serves 2
Preparation time 5 minutes
Cooking time 4–5 minutes

This sandwich brings all the flavors and scents of Italy flooding into your kitchen. The simple, fresh blend of these ingredients will change your opinion of the humble tuna sandwich forever.

1 Spread the pesto evenly over each ciabatta base. Top with the tuna and the boccocini halves. Drizzle the oil and balsamic vinegar over them and finish with the basil leaves and sun-dried tomatoes.

2 Top with the lids and toast in a sandwich grill for 4–5 minutes, or according to the manufacturer's instructions, until they are golden and crispy.

miso tuna and wilted greens

2 tuna steaks, about 6 oz each
1/4 cup miso soup paste
1 head of bok choy, halved
2 pita breads, cut in half horizontally
large handful of baby spinach leaves
1 teaspoon sesame oil

Serves 2
Preparation time 4 minutes,
plus marinating
Cooking time 6 minutes

1 Rub the tuna steaks all over with the miso soup paste and set aside for at least 20 minutes to marinate. Preheat a frying pan and cook the tuna for 3–4 minutes, turning once, until almost cooked. Add the halves of bok choy, cut side down, for the last 2 minutes of cooking time.

2 Remove both the tuna and the bok choy and arrange them on the bases of the pita breads. Toss the spinach leaves in the sesame oil and place on top of the tuna. Top with the lids then toast in a sandwich grill for 1–2 minutes, or according to the manufacturer's instructions, until the bread is crispy and the spinach has wilted.

teriyaki salmon with wasabi dressing

2 salmon fillets, about 6 oz each
2 large sesame seed buns, cut in half
   horizontally
1 scallion (green onion), finely sliced
finely shredded cucumber, to serve

Teriyaki sauce
1/4 cup soy sauce
1/2 cup sake
1/2 cup mirin
2 tablespoons light brown sugar
1 2-inch cube fresh root ginger, peeled
   and finely shredded
1 garlic clove, chopped

Wasabi dressing
1 teaspoon sesame oil
1 teaspoon wasabi paste
2 tablespoons superfine sugar
2 teaspoons soy sauce
1/3 cup rice wine vinegar

Serves 2
Preparation time 8–10 minutes,
plus marinating
Cooking time 12 minutes

If you're short on time, you can always buy the teriyaki sauce at the supermarket, but this homemade recipe is easy and delicious, and the sauce can be kept in a refrigerator for several weeks.

1 Make the teriyaki sauce. Place all the ingredients in a small pan and heat gently until the sugar dissolves completely. Remove from the heat. Once the sauce is cold, place the salmon fillets in a shallow dish with the sauce and leave to marinate for between 30 minutes and 1 hour.

2 Transfer the salmon fillets and teriyaki sauce into a heated frying pan and cook the fillets over medium heat for 2–3 minutes each side, basting frequently with the sauce, until they are almost cooked.

3 Lift the salmon from the pan onto the sesame seed bun bases. Top with the lids and toast in a sandwich grill for 2–3 minutes, or according to the manufacturer's instructions, until the bread is golden and crispy. Remove from the sandwich grill and cut each sandwich into canapé-sized pieces.

4 Meanwhile, combine the wasabi dressing ingredients in a screw-top jar. Pour the dressing into little dipping dishes and sprinkle with the sliced scallion (green onion). Serve immediately with the salmon sandwiches and shredded cucumber.

breaded fish and crushed peas

1 cup frozen petite peas
2 tablespoons butter
1/4 cup finely chopped mint
1/4 cup fresh breadcrumbs
finely grated zest of 1 lemon
1/4 cup chopped parsley
1 large egg, lightly beaten
2 fish fillets (cod, lemon sole, or any
    white flaky fish), about 4 oz each
1/3 cup vegetable oil
2 large, soft, floured rolls, cut in half
    horizontally
salt and pepper
tartar sauce, to serve

Serves 2
Preparation time 12 minutes
Cooking time 10–12 minutes

1 Bring a pan of salted water to a rolling boil and cook the peas for about 4 minutes until they are soft. Drain and return to the pan with the butter and some salt and pepper. Use a potato masher to crush the peas so that they are almost puréed. Stir in the chopped mint and set aside.

2 Mix the breadcrumbs with the lemon zest, some salt and pepper, and the chopped parsley, and spread on a large plate. Pour the beaten egg into a shallow bowl and dip the fish fillets into it before placing them on the breadcrumbs. Turn the fish in the breadcrumbs, making sure that the flesh is completely covered.

3 Heat the oil in a medium-sized frying pan and lay the fish in the pan over medium-high heat. Cook for about 4 minutes, turning once, until the fish is cooked through and the breadcrumbs are golden and crispy.

4 Spread the crushed peas over the bases of the rolls and lay the fish on top. Top with the lids then toast in a sandwich grill for 2–3 minutes, or according to the manufacturer's instructions, until the bread is golden and crispy. Cut each sandwich into quarters and serve immediately with tartar sauce.

buttered shrimp

2 tablespoons butter
7 oz shrimp, preferably gulf shrimp,
    cooked and peeled
1/3 cup roughly chopped parsley
pinch of cayenne pepper
pinch of freshly ground nutmeg
pinch of ground mace
1 teaspoon lemon juice
1 teaspoon grated fresh root ginger
4 chapattis
curly endive salad, to serve

Serves 2
Preparation time 5 minutes
Cooking time 8 minutes

This recipe is inspired by a traditional English favorite, potted shrimp. The recipe goes well with chapattis but is also good with any other whole-wheat flat bread.

1 Place the butter in a frying pan and warm over medium heat until it is melted and beginning to froth. Stir in the shrimp, followed by the parsley, spices, lemon juice, and ginger, and cook for 2–3 minutes until the butter turns golden.

2 Spoon the mixture over two of the chapattis and top with the remaining chapattis. Toast in a sandwich grill for 2–3 minutes, or according to the manufacturer's instructions, until the chapattis are golden and crispy. Serve immediately with a curly endive salad.

crispy seaweed and shrimp

oil, for deep frying
6 sheets dried nori seaweed,
    finely shredded
7 oz shrimp, cooked and peeled
1/2 teaspoon crushed red pepper flakes
    (optional)
2 tablespoons toasted sesame seeds
2 tablespoons chili oil
1 2-inch cube fresh root ginger, peeled
    and finely shredded
4 taco-size tortillas
soy sauce, to serve

Serves 2
Preparation time 5 minutes
Cooking time 4 minutes

1 Heat the oil in a deep frying pan to 350° or until a cube of bread dropped in the pan browns in 20 seconds. Carefully drop the seaweed into the oil for a few seconds, scooping it out with a large slotted spoon as soon as it goes crispy. Drain on plenty of paper towels to get rid of excess oil and set aside.

2 In a bowl toss together the shrimp, red pepper flakes (if using), sesame seeds, chili oil, and shredded ginger. Place the mixture on the tortillas, covering half of each one, and fold over the other half to enclose the shrimp mixture.

3 Toast in a sandwich grill for 2–3 minutes, or according to the manufacturer's instructions, until hot and crispy. Cut each tortilla crescent into three equal pieces and serve immediately with the crispy seaweed and a bowl of soy sauce.

anchovy, artichoke, and radicchio puff

3 oz fresh, cooked, marinated deli-style
anchovies (drained weight)

4 oz marinated baby artichokes,
drained and thickly sliced

1 small head of radicchio, leaves
separated

1/2 small red onion, finely sliced

1/3 cup finely grated pecorino cheese

2 tablespoons chopped chervil

pepper

7 oz ready-to-bake rolled puff pastry,
cut into 2 rectangles, each
8 x 6 inches

To serve
lemony mayonnaise
green salad

Serves 2
Preparation time 8 minutes
Cooking time 5–6 minutes

Not all sandwiches have to use bread as a base. In this parcel, delicate layers of puff pastry encase a delicious filling.

1   Arrange all the ingredients in the middle of the two rectangles of puff pastry. Fold over and press to seal in the filling so that you are left with two parcels.

2   Toast the parcels in a sandwich grill for 5–6 minutes, or according to the manufacturer's instructions, until the pastry is cooked and golden and the filling is hot. Serve immediately with a lemony mayonnaise and a green salad.

cilantro and chili crab

4 phyllo pastry sheets, about 8 x 12
   inches each
1/4 cup melted butter

Crab filling
1 lemon grass stalk
1 6-oz can crab meat, drained, or 6 oz
   fresh cooked crab meat
finely grated zest of 1 lime
4 tablespoons chopped cilantro leaves
   and stems
2 tablespoons chopped mint
2 tablespoons lime juice
1 small red chile, seeded and finely
   chopped
2 tablespoons fish sauce
1/2 teaspoon palm sugar
salt and pepper

Serves 2
Preparation time 12 minutes
Cooking time 3–4 minutes

Phyllo pastry works wonderfully to make this zingy crab parcel.

1 Make the crab filling. Strip the lemon grass stalk of its outer layers and finely slice the soft heart. Mix it in a bowl together with all the remaining crab filling ingredients, season, and set aside.

2 Brush each sheet of filo pastry with melted butter and arrange two of them crosswise over each other. Repeat with the remaining two sheets.

3 Spoon the crab mixture into the middle of each pastry arrangement and fold over the sides to create neat parcels.

4 Toast in a sandwich grill for 3–4 minutes, or according to the manufacturer's instructions, until the pastry is golden and crispy. Serve immediately.

a meaty offering

super club with grain mustard

1/4 cup mayonnaise, plus extra to serve
2 tablespoons wholegrain mustard,
    plus extra to serve
4 slices of multigrain bread
2 slices of honey-roast ham
3 oz deli-style turkey, in wafer-thin
    slices
3 oz sharp Cheddar cheese, finely
    sliced
1 large beefsteak tomato, sliced
1/2 small red onion, finely sliced
6 slices of cooked, smoked bacon
6 French-style cornichons or
    American-style gherkins, finely
    sliced (optional)
2 tablespoons chopped chives

Serves 2
Preparation time 5 minutes
Cooking time 3–4 minutes

1 Combine the mayonnaise and mustard in a small bowl and spread the mixture over one side of each slice of multigrain bread. Arrange the ham slices on two slices of bread, followed by the sliced turkey. Top with the Cheddar and tomato and scatter with the red onion. Next, top with the bacon and cornichon or gherkin slices (if using), then sprinkle the chives over the filling before covering with the remaining two slices of bread.

2 Toast in a sandwich grill for 3–4 minutes, or according to the manufacturer's instructions, until the filling is hot and melting and the bread is golden. Serve immediately with extra mayonnaise and mustard sauce and plenty of napkins!

mexican chili beef

14 oz sirloin steak
4 taco-size tomato and herb tortillas
3 oz mild Cheddar cheese, grated
1 red onion, finely sliced
2 jalapeño peppers, sliced (optional)

Mexican spice
1 teaspoon dried Mexican oregano
1/2 teaspoon dried garlic
1 teaspoon dried onion
1/4 teaspoon dried chili powder
2 tablespoons crushed red pepper
   flakes
1/2 teaspoon dried chili flakes
1/4 teaspoon ground cumin
1/4 teaspoon ground coriander
salt and pepper

To serve
sour cream
guacamole
salsa

Serves 2
Preparation time 8 minutes
Cooking time 4–9 minutes

1 Combine the Mexican spice ingredients together and rub the mixture generously into the steak. Place the steak directly on a sandwich grill and bring down the top plate to seal it. Cook for about 2 minutes for a rare steak, 2 minutes longer for medium, and a further 2 minutes if you like your steak well done. Remove from the heat and set aside.

2 When the meat is cool enough to handle, slice it finely and arrange in the middle of the four tortillas. Sprinkle with the grated Cheddar, red onion, and sliced jalapeños (if using). Fold over the sides of the tortillas to cover the filling.

3 Toast the tortillas in the sandwich grill for 2–3 minutes, or according to the manufacturer's instructions, until they are crispy and the filling is hot. Serve immediately with sour cream, guacamole, and salsa.

philly cheese steak

1/4 cup olive oil

1/2 red bell pepper, cored and finely sliced

1/2 green bell pepper, cored and finely sliced

1 small onion, halved and finely sliced

10 oz rib-eye steak, finely sliced

1 cup mushrooms, trimmed and sliced

1 garlic clove, chopped

3 oz provolone cheese, finely sliced

2 tablespoons Worcestershire or steak sauce

4 long slices of French country bread

1 dill pickle, finely sliced (optional)

salt and pepper

To serve
cherry tomatoes

Serves 2
Preparation time 8 minutes
Cooking time 12–15 minutes

1 Heat the olive oil in a frying pan and add the peppers and onion. Cook over medium-high heat for 3–4 minutes until they just begin to soften. Add the steak and continue cooking for 2–3 minutes before adding the mushrooms and garlic. Cook for a further 3–4 minutes.

2 Reduce the heat to low, season well, and then use two wooden spatulas to form the steak mixture into two piles, roughly the size of the bread slices. Place the slices of cheese on top of each pile and leave to melt for 2 minutes.

3 Spread a little of the Worcestershire or steak sauce over two slices of bread and then very carefully lift the cheese-steak mixture onto the French country bread, again using two spatulas. Splash the remaining sauce over the mixture and arrange the pickle slices on top (if using).

4 Top with the two remaining bread slices to form two sandwiches and toast in a sandwich grill for 2–3 minutes, or according to the manufacturer's instructions, until the bread is crispy and the cheese is completely melted. Serve immediately with a bowl of cherry tomatoes.

pastrami with red onion chutney

4 slices of rye bread
5 oz shaved pastrami
2 slices of sharp Cheddar cheese
barbecue sauce, to serve

Chutney
2 tablespoons butter
2 tablespoons chili oil
2 red onions, sliced
1 teaspoon black mustard seeds
2 tablespoons sherry vinegar
salt and pepper

Serves 2
Preparation time 8 minutes
Cooking time 18–19 minutes

1 Make the chutney. Heat the butter and chili oil in a frying pan and add the onions and mustard seeds. Fry gently over low heat for about 15 minutes until the onions are soft and lightly golden in color. Stir in the sherry vinegar, season well, and set aside to cool.

2 Spoon the onion chutney onto two slices of rye bread and layer the shaved pastrami on top. Place the slices of Cheddar on the pastrami and top with the lids. Toast in a sandwich grill for 3–4 minutes, or according to the manufacturer's instructions, until the bread is toasted and the cheese has melted. Serve immediately with barbecue sauce.

egyptian-spiced lamb

2/3 cup olive oil
1 eggplant, cut into 1/2-inch slices
1 large onion, finely sliced
11 oz ground lamb
1/4 cup lemon juice
1/4 cup chopped mint
1 large Eastern-style sesame bread,
   cut in half and sliced horizontally
Greek yogurt with chopped mint,
   to serve

Dukka seasoning
1/2 cup walnuts
1/4 cup sesame seeds
2 tablespoons coriander seeds
2 tablespoons cumin seeds
1/2 teaspoon dried mint
1/2 teaspoon black peppercorns
1 teaspoon salt

Serves 2
Preparation time 12 minutes
Cooking time 21–25 minutes

You can double the amounts of this Egyptian dukka seasoning and store it in an airtight container for about 3 weeks.

1 Make the dukka seasoning. Place the walnuts, sesame seeds, coriander seeds, and cumin seeds in a heavy-based frying pan and dry-roast gently over medium-low heat for 3–4 minutes. Allow to cool, then combine with the remaining ingredients. Transfer to a spice grinder and process into a coarse powder.

2 Heat 1/3 cup of the oil in a large frying pan and fry the eggplant slices over medium-high heat for about 2 minutes on each side, until golden. Remove the eggplant slices from the pan and drain on plenty of paper towels to get rid of excess oil.

3 Add the remaining oil to the pan and toss in the onion slices, frying over medium heat for 5–6 minutes until soft and golden. Add the lamb and 1/2 cup of the spice mix and fry for 5–6 minutes until the meat is browned. Stir in the lemon juice and chopped mint.

4 Layer the eggplant slices on the sesame bread bases and spoon the lamb mixture over them. Top with the lids and toast in a sandwich grill for 4–5 minutes, or according to the manufacturer's instructions, until the bread is golden and the filling is hot. Serve immediately with fresh minty yogurt.

smoky bacon, tomato, and avocado

4 oz mozzarella cheese, sliced

4 slices of Irish soda bread

4 slices of cooked Irish-style bacon

1 small avocado, peeled, pitted, and
   sliced

8 cherry tomatoes, halved

2 scallions (green onions), finely sliced

2 tablespoons basil oil

pepper

Serves 2
Preparation time 5 minutes
Cooking time 3–4 minutes

1 Arrange the mozzarella slices over two slices of soda bread. Top with the bacon, avocado, and halved cherry tomatoes. Sprinkle with the sliced scallions (green onions) and drizzle with basil oil. Season well with freshly ground black pepper and top with the remaining bread.

2 Toast the sandwiches in a sandwich grill for 3–4 minutes, or according to the manufacturer's instructions, until the bread is golden and the cheese is melting.

pizza lover's grilled sandwich

1 small package pizza dough mix or
   2 pieces of onion foccacia cut in half
   horizontally
2 ripe plum tomatoes, finely sliced
4 thin slices of prosciutto
3 marinated artichokes, halved
4 oz smoked mozzarella cheese, sliced
2 tablespoons olive oil
1 teaspoon dried oregano
tomato salad, to serve

Serves 2
Preparation time 6 minutes, plus
making the pizza dough
Cooking time 4–5 minutes

Using pizza dough for this recipe works fantastically well, creating a type of flat, calzone-style pizza. The choice of possible fillings is endless. If you are short on time, but like the idea, use onion foccacia in place of the dough.

1 Make the pizza dough according to package instructions. Roll it into two thin circles. Cover one half of each dough circle with the tomatoes, prosciutto, artichokes, and mozzarella. Drizzle with olive oil and sprinkle with oregano. Fold over the dough to encase the toppings, like two calzone-style pizzas.

2 Toast the pizzas in a sandwich grill for 4–5 minutes, or according to the manufacturer's instructions, until the dough is crispy and golden and the filling is hot and melted. Serve immediately with a simple tomato salad.

pork tenderloin medallions with apple

1/3 cup olive oil
10 oz pork tenderloin, finely sliced
1/4 cup hard cider
1/4 cup cider vinegar
2 shallots, finely chopped
2 teaspoons chopped thyme
1 bay leaf
1/3 cup crème fraîche
2 tablespoons butter
1 apple, cored and sliced
7 oz ready-to-bake rolled puff pastry,
   cut into 2 6-inch squares
salt and pepper
arugula, to garnish

Serves 2
Preparation time 10 minutes
Cooking time 18 minutes

1 Heat 1/4 cup of the olive oil in a large frying pan and fry the pork slices until golden. Pour in half the cider and the cider vinegar and heat until the liquid bubbles and evaporates. Remove the pork from the pan and set aside. Wipe the pan with a paper towel and add a teaspoon of the olive oil. Put the shallots in the pan and return it to the heat, frying gently until soft and golden. Add 1 teaspoon of the thyme, the bay leaf, crème fraîche, and the remaining cider, and season. Reserve the sauce and keep warm.

2 In a separate frying pan, heat the butter and the remaining olive oil. Add the apple slices and fry over medium-high heat until golden and caramelized. Remove with a slotted spoon and drain on paper towels.

3 Imagine there is a diagonal line through the pastry squares and arrange the apple and pork slices over one side of the line, sprinkle with the remaining thyme, season well, and fold to form two triangular parcels. Toast in a sandwich grill for 5–6 minutes, or according to the manufacturer's instructions, until the pastry is golden and crisp. Serve immediately with the reserved sauce and garnish with arugula.

black forest ham, cheese, and asparagus

4 thin slices of Black Forest ham

3 oz fontina cheese, grated

small handful of arugula

4 oz trimmed asparagus spears, steamed

2 vine-ripened tomatoes, sliced

4 slices of sourdough bread

2 tablespoons olive oil

2 teaspoons balsamic vinegar

Serves 2
Preparation time 5 minutes
Cooking time 3–4 minutes

Steam the asparagus so that it is still firm—the slight crunch contrasts wonderfully with the oozing melted cheese.

1 Arrange the ham, grated fontina, arugula, asparagus, and tomatoes over two slices of sourdough bread. Drizzle with the olive oil and balsamic vinegar and top with the lids.

2 Toast the sandwiches in a sandwich grill for 3–4 minutes, or according to the manufacturer's instructions, until the bread is golden and the cheese has melted. Serve immediately.

lima bean and chorizo crostini

1 cup cooked lima beans

2 oz chorizo sausage, finely shredded

2 tablespoons lightly toasted pine nuts
(optional)

1/4 cup finely chopped parsley

2 teaspoons lemon juice

finely grated zest of half a lemon

1/2 teaspoon smoked paprika

4 large slices of Italian-style country
bread

2 tablespoons olive oil

salt and pepper

green salad, to serve

Serves 2

Preparation time 5 minutes, plus
marinating

Cooking time 4–5 minutes

*The olive oil-brushed bread turns this sandwich into a Spanish-style crostini,
reminiscent of the tapas you find in Spanish street cafés.*

1 Mix all the ingredients except the bread, olive oil, and salad together in a bowl,
season to taste, and leave to marinate for about 10 minutes. This allows the
flavors to develop and enables any juices to be soaked up into the beans, which
keeps the bread from getting too wet.

2 Brush one side of two slices of Italian-style country bread with a little olive oil,
and then spoon the filling onto the dry sides. Top each with another slice of
bread, brush the tops with a little olive oil, and place on a sandwich grill. Bring
down the top and toast for 4–5 minutes, or according to the manufacturer's
instructions, until the bread is golden and crispy. Cut in half diagonally and serve
immediately with a green salad.

smoked chicken with crispy pancetta

4 thin slices of pancetta
2 onion bagels, cut in half horizontally
3 oz firm Brie, sliced
3 1/2 oz cooked, smoked chicken breast,
   shredded
4–5 sage leaves

Serves 2
Preparation time 3 minutes
Cooking time 8–10 minutes

This can be made on any kind of bread—wholegrain works well—but somehow onion bagels seem to make it the perfect comfort food.

1 Preheat the sandwich grill and place the slices of pancetta inside for about 2 minutes, until golden and crispy. Remove and set aside on paper towels. Wipe the machine with a damp cloth.

2 Place the bagels, cut side down, on the sandwich grill and cook for 2–3 minutes, without bringing down the top plate, until golden and toasted. Remove and arrange the Brie, chicken breast, and pancetta on the base of the bagels. Scatter the sage leaves over it and top with the lids.

3 Toast the bagels in the sandwich grill for 4–5 minutes, or according to the manufacturer's instructions, until the bread is golden and crispy and the filling is melting. Serve immediately.

roasted rosemary chicken

2 chicken breasts, about 5 oz each
2 teaspoons tapenade
4 sun-dried tomatoes
1 garlic clove, cut into slivers
3–4 sprigs of rosemary
2 tablespoons olive oil
2 large wholegrain rolls, cut in half
  horizontally
2 oz pecorino cheese, shaved
salt and pepper
arugula, to garnish

Serves 2
Preparation time 8 minutes
Cooking time 22 minutes

1 Using a sharp knife, make a horizontal slit in each chicken breast. Do not cut all the way through but just deep enough to create a pocket in the flesh. Stuff the tapenade, sun-dried tomatoes, and garlic slivers into the pocket and close it up. Lay the chicken breasts on top of the rosemary sprigs in a roasting pan and drizzle with olive oil. Season with a little salt and pepper and cook in a preheated 350° oven for about 18 minutes, until the chicken is cooked through.

2 When the chicken is cool enough to handle, cut it into slices. Arrange the meat on the wholegrain roll bases, sprinkle with the pecorino shavings, and top with the lids. Toast in a sandwich grill for 3–4 minutes, or according to the manufacturer's instructions, until the bread is golden and the chicken is hot. Serve immediately garnished with arugula.

chicken caesar

2 tablespoons olive oil

4 slices of bacon

4 oz cooked chicken breast, sliced

1 small wholegrain baguette, cut in half
horizontally

1/3 cup prepared creamy Caesar
dressing, plus extra to serve

4 anchovies in olive oil, drained
(optional)

1 oz Parmesan cheese, shaved

Bibb or other butter lettuce, to serve

Serves 2
Preparation time 5 minutes
Cooking time 7–9 minutes

1 Heat a small frying pan over medium heat and add the olive oil. Place the bacon in the pan and fry for 2–3 minutes, turning once, until crisp and golden.

2 Layer the slices of chicken breast on the base of the wholegrain baguette and top with the bacon. Drizzle with the Caesar dressing and top with the anchovies (if using) and the Parmesan shavings.

3 Put the top of the baguette over the filling, slice into two equal halves, and place in a sandwich grill. Toast for 5–6 minutes, or according to the manufacturer's instructions, until the sandwiches are hot throughout and golden and crispy.

4 Serve the sandwiches immediately together with the lettuce and some extra creamy Caesar dressing for drizzling.

thai red chicken

10 oz boneless chicken thighs, thickly
   sliced
1/3 cup Thai red curry paste
2 pita breads, split in half horizontally

Satay sauce
1 cup cashew nuts, lightly toasted
1 teaspoon crushed red pepper flakes
1/4 cup soy sauce
1 cup coconut milk
1/4 cup cilantro leaves, plus extra
   to garnish
2 tablespoons palm sugar or light
   brown sugar
2 tablespoons rice wine vinegar
2 kaffir lime leaves, shredded
2 tablespoons peanut oil

Serves 2
Preparation time 8 minutes
Cooking time 9–12 minutes

Leftover satay sauce can be kept for at least a week in a screw-top jar in the refrigerator—but it may be too delicious to last!

1 To make the satay sauce, place the nuts in a food processor and pulse until finely chopped. Place in a small pan with the remaining satay ingredients and heat gently for 4–5 minutes, stirring frequently to prevent sticking, until the sauce is thick and glossy.

2 Mix the chicken thighs with the red curry paste and thread onto four metal skewers. Preheat the sandwich grill and lay the skewers directly on the heat, bringing down the top plate to seal the chicken. Grill for 4–5 minutes, until the chicken is thoroughly cooked. Remove from the heat and set aside.

3 When the meat is cool enough to handle, push the chicken off the skewers directly into the pita breads. Toast the breads in the cleaned sandwich grill for 1–2 minutes, or according to the manufacturer's instructions, until they are crispy and the chicken hot. Cut each pita in half and serve immediately with a bowl of the warm cashew satay sauce and a garnish of cilantro leaves.

spicy tandoori chicken

2 chicken breasts, about 4 oz each
1/4 cup mango chutney
2 naan breads, split in half horizontally
1/4 cup roughly chopped cilantro leaves

Marinade
1 cup Greek yogurt
1 garlic clove, crushed
1 teaspoon ground coriander seeds
pinch of ground turmeric
1/2 teaspoon hot chili powder
2 teaspoons tandoori masala
1 teaspoon garam masala
1 teaspoon ground cumin
1/4 cup lemon juice
2 tablespoons olive oil
salt and pepper

To serve
sliced cucumber
Greek yogurt

Serves 2
Preparation time 8 minutes, plus
marinating
Cooking time 25 minutes

This is so good that you may never buy another sandwich again!

1 Make three or four slashes in each chicken breast and set them aside in a bowl. Mix together all the marinade ingredients in another bowl and pour the mixture over the chicken. Cover and leave to marinate in the refrigerator for at least 4 hours, but preferably overnight.

2 Take the chicken out of the marinade and place it directly on a baking sheet. Cook in a preheated 400° oven for about 20 minutes, until the chicken is cooked through. Remove from the oven and leave to cool.

3 Spread the mango chutney over half of each naan bread. Cut the chicken into thick slices and arrange the meat on the base of each naan. Scatter the cilantro leaves over it and cover with the lids. Toast in a sandwich grill for 4–5 minutes, or according to the manufacturer's instructions, until the bread is golden and crispy and the filling is hot. Serve immediately with cucumber slices and Greek yogurt.

turkey and cranberry sauce

1/3 cup cranberry sauce
 (made from whole berries)
4 slices of corn bread
3/4 cup corn kernels
4 oz smoked turkey breast, finely sliced

Serves 2
Preparation time 2 minutes
Cooking time 2–3 minutes

1 Spread the cranberry sauce over two slices of corn bread. Scatter the corn kernels over it, then top with the smoked turkey.

2 Top with the lids and toast in a sandwich grill for 2–3 minutes, or according to the manufacturer's instructions, until the bread is golden and crispy.

sliced duck breast

1/4 cup honey

1/4 cup dark soy sauce

1 teaspoon five spice powder

2 duck breasts, about 5 oz each

1/4 cup hoisin sauce, plus extra
   to serve

4 taco-size tortillas

2 scallions (green onions), sliced
   lengthwise

sliced cucumber, to serve

Serves 2
Preparation time 10 minutes
Cooking time 7–9 minutes

If your favorite item on the menu of your local Chinese restaurant is the crispy duck pancake, you are sure to love this recipe. Bringing the takeout to you!

1   In a small bowl combine the honey, soy sauce, and five spice powder. Use a sharp knife to make three or four cuts in each duck breast and rub the honey mixture generously over the meat, making sure it gets into each cut.

2   Heat the sandwich grill and place the duck breasts inside, pushing the top plate down heavily. Leave to cook for 5–6 minutes, until the outsides of the duck breasts are crispy and golden and the insides are almost cooked. Remove and set aside to cool. Wipe the machine with a damp cloth.

3   Use a sharp knife to slice the duck breasts finely. Spread a little hoisin sauce over the base of each tortilla. Arrange the duck on the sauce over half of each tortilla base and then scatter the sliced scallions (green onions) over it.

4   Fold the tortillas in half and toast in the sandwich grill for 2–3 minutes or according to the manufacturer's instructions, until they are golden and crispy. Serve immediately with cucumber slices and extra hoisin sauce.

all things sweet

melting ice cream and raspberries

1 cup raspberries

finely grated zest of 1 orange

2 tablespoons orange juice

2 tablespoons kirsch

2 tablespoons orange blossom honey

2 large English tea cakes or blueberry
    bagels, cut in half horizontally

2 large scoops vanilla-raspberry swirl
    ice cream, to serve

Serves 2
Preparation time 3 minutes
Cooking time 2–3 minutes

1 In a large bowl toss together the raspberries, grated orange zest and juice, kirsch, and orange blossom honey.

2 Spoon the raspberry mixture onto the tea cake or bagel bases, top with the lids, and toast in a sandwich grill for 2–3 minutes, or according to the manufacturer's instructions, until golden and crispy.

3 Cut each grilled sandwich into thin slices. Serve immediately with a scoop of vanilla-raspberry swirl ice cream.

cinnamon, mascarpone, and amaretti

1/2 cup mascarpone cheese
1 teaspoon ground cinnamon
1/4 cup maple syrup
1/4 cup Amaretto liqueur
4 slices of panettone
1/2 cup amaretti cookies, crushed

Serves 2
Preparation time 5 minutes
Cooking time 2–3 minutes

The crunch of amaretti cookies contrasts perfectly with the silky smoothness of the sweet cinnamon mascarpone.

1 Thoroughly mix together the mascarpone, cinnamon, maple syrup, and the liqueur. Spread over two slices of panettone, scatter the crushed cookies over it and then top with the remaining slices of panettone.

2 Toast in a sandwich grill for 2–3 minutes, or according to the manufacturer's instructions, until the bread is toasted and the filling is beginning to ooze from the sides. Serve immediately.

jordan almond and mascarpone

3¹/2 oz marzipan, chopped
4 dessert crêpes
3/4 cup Jordan almonds, crushed

To serve
mascarpone
honey
lemon juice

Serves 2
Preparation time 3 minutes
Cooking time 1–2 minutes

Jordan almonds, (also known as sugared almonds), are almonds encased in hard pastel candy coatings of various colors. They are available in Italian delicatessens. A tasty alternative to mascarpone in this recipe is Devonshire clotted cream, available in specialist food stores.

1 Scatter the chopped marzipan over half of each crêpe and then sprinkle with the crushed Jordan almonds.

2 Fold the crêpes in half and in half again and toast in a sandwich grill for 1–2 minutes, or according to the manufacturer's instructions, until they are hot and the marzipan is melting.

3 Serve immediately topped with a dollop of mascarpone, a drizzle of honey, and a squeeze of lemon juice.

mango and mint with warm blackberry coulis

1 1/2 cups blackberries

1/3 cup superfine sugar

2 tablespoons cassis liqueur (at least
  16% alcohol)

4 thick slices of all-butter brioche

1 small, ripe mango, pitted, peeled,
  and finely sliced

6–8 small mint leaves, shredded

confectioners' sugar, to decorate

To serve
crème fraîche
2 sprigs of mint

Serves 2
Preparation time 8 minutes
Cooking time 10–12 minutes

1 In a small pan gently warm 1 cup of the blackberries with 1/4 cup sugar and 2 tablespoons of cold water until the sugar dissolves completely. Allow the mixture to bubble gently so that the blackberries collapse, creating a thick fruity liquid. Remove from the heat and leave to cool. Use a blender to purée into a rich, smooth coulis, stir in the cassis, and set aside.

2 Sprinkle 1 tablespoon of the sugar over two slices of brioche. Arrange the mango slices on top and then scatter the shredded mint leaves and remaining blackberries over them. Top with the lids and sprinkle the surface with the remaining sugar.

3 Toast in a sandwich grill for 2–3 minutes, or according to the manufacturer's instructions, until the bread is golden and crispy. Cut the sandwiches in half and serve immediately with a drizzle of the warm coulis, some crème fraîche, sprigs of mint, and a dusting of confectioners' sugar.

ginger, chocolate, and banana parcels

4 sheets phyllo pastry, each 8 x 12
   inches
1/4 cup melted butter
1 large banana, sliced lengthwise
3 oz dark chocolate, chopped
1/2 cup pecan halves, roughly chopped
1/4 cup dark brown sugar
1/2 teaspoon ground ginger
pinch of apple-pie spice
vanilla ice cream, to serve

Serves 2
Preparation time 8 minutes
Cooking time 3–4 minutes

If you are in the mood for comfort food, look no further!

1 Brush the sheets of phyllo with the melted butter and arrange them in two stacks of two sheets. Arrange the banana in the middle of each stack, scatter with the chopped chocolate and pecans, and sprinkle with the sugar and spices.

2 Fold over the sides of the phyllo pastry to form two parcels and toast in a sandwich grill for 3–4 minutes, or according to the manufacturer's instructions, until the pastry is crisp and golden. Serve hot, with a scoop of vanilla ice cream.

crunchy lemon cream and sponge toffee

1/4 cup heavy cream, plus extra to
  serve
11/2 oz sponge toffee, crumbled
1 teaspoon finely grated lemon zest
1/4 cup candied lemon peel, finely
  chopped (optional)
1/3 cup traditional lemon curd
6 Scotch pancakes
blueberries, to serve

Serves 2
Preparation time 6 minutes
Cooking time 1–2 minutes

This is a lovely, fresh, summery dessert—wonderful enjoyed with a chilled glass of tart, homemade lemonade. Sponge toffee is known by many names around the world—honeycomb, cinder toffee, sponge candy, hokey pokey, toffee honeycomb, puff candy, and seafoam candy.

1 In a bowl combine the cream, sponge toffee, lemon zest, candied peel (if using), and lemon curd. Place a dollop of the lemon cream on a pancake, top with a second pancake and another dollop of lemon cream on top then finish with a third pancake. Repeat the process so that you are left with two triple-decker lemon pancakes.

2 Toast the pancake stacks in a sandwich grill for 1–2 minutes, or according to the manufacturer's instructions, until the outside pancakes are toasted and the lemon cream is beginning to ooze from the sides. Serve immediately with some blueberries.

manchego and figs

2 thick slices of manchego cheese
2 ripe figs, cut into quarters
4 slices of pumpernickel bread

Serves 2
Preparation time 2 minutes
Cooking time 2–3 minutes

Use the best possible ingredients in this simple cheese-course dessert.

1 Arrange the slices of manchego and the fig quarters on two slices of pumpernickel bread and top with the lids.

2 Toast the sandwiches in a sandwich grill for 2–3 minutes, or according to the manufacturer's instructions, until the bread is toasted and the cheese is melting. Serve immediately.

triple chocolate chunk

4 slices of Italian country-style bread
3 oz milk chocolate, chopped
3 oz dark chocolate, chopped
3 oz white chocolate, chopped
1/4 cup toasted hazelnuts, roughly
    chopped (optional)

Serves 2
Preparation time 2 minutes
Cooking time 2–3 minutes

You should choose country-style bread for this recipe so that the chewy toast contrasts with the melted chocolate.

1 Scatter two slices of country-style bread with the chocolate chunks and the hazelnuts (if using) and top with the remaining two slices of bread.

2 Toast in a sandwich grill for 2–3 minutes, or according to the manufacturer's instructions, until the bread is golden and toasted and the chocolate has begun to melt. Serve immediately.

hot irish coffee

2 tablespoons superfine sugar
1/4 cup espresso coffee
2 tablespoons whiskey or Irish coffee-
    flavored syrup
4 slices of crusty white bread
1/2 cup chocolate chips
1/4 cup mascarpone cheese
cocoa powder, to decorate
lightly whipped cream, to serve

Serves 2
Preparation time 5 minutes
Cooking time 2–3 minutes

This delicious creation is like a cross between a hot Irish coffee and a tiramisu in a sandwich—pure luxury!

1 Stir the sugar into the hot coffee and mix with the whiskey or Irish coffee-flavored syrup. Dip two slices of the crusty bread into the mixture and scatter the chocolate chips over them. Spread the mascarpone over the remaining slices of bread and place them on top of the chocolate chips.

2 Toast in a sandwich grill for 2–3 minutes, or according to the manufacturer's instructions, until the bread is crisp. Dust with cocoa powder and serve immediately with a dollop of lightly whipped cream.

pineapple and sticky macadamia nuts

4 pineapple rings in juice, drained
4 slices of panettone
1/3 cup mini-marshmallows
1/4 cup macadamia nuts, crushed
2 tablespoons vanilla sugar
confectioners' sugar, to decorate

Serves 2
Preparation time 4 minutes
Cooking time 2–3 minutes

*Don't be fooled by the grown-up sounding title—this is not an adult dessert;
it is strictly for the kids among us!*

1 Pat the pineapple rings dry on paper towels and arrange them on two slices of panettone. Scatter with the marshmallows and crushed macadamia nuts and sprinkle with the vanilla sugar. Top with the remaining two slices of bread.

2 Toast in a sandwich grill for 2–3 minutes, or according to the manufacturer's instructions, until the bread is golden and the marshmallows are beginning to melt. Slice each sandwich into small rectangles and dust with confectioners' sugar. Serve immediately.

index

acknowledgments

Executive editor Sarah Ford
Editor Leanne Bryan
Executive art editor Jo MacGregor
Designer Darren Southern
Photographer Lis Parsons
Home economist Emma Jane Frost
Stylist Rachel Jukes
Production controller Nigel Reed
Picture researcher Sophie Delpech